T0150757

Also by **IVAN DRURY**

As editor and contributor
Red Braid, *A Separate Star: Politics and Strategy in
Anti-Colonial, Anti-Capitalist, and Anti-Imperialist Struggle*

Ivan Drury

5

POEMS

 TALONBOOKS

Talonbooks
9259 Shaughnessy Street, Vancouver, British Columbia, Canada V6P 6R4
talonbooks.com

Talonbooks is located on xʷməθkʷəy̓əm, Sk̲wx̲wú7mesh, and səl̓ilwətaʔɬ Lands.

First printing: 2022

Typeset in Avenir
Printed and bound in Canada on 100% post-consumer recycled paper

Interior design by Typesmith
On the back cover and inside cover: *Guantánamo Sea* by Ivan Drury
Cover by Typesmith with Ivan Drury

Talonbooks acknowledges the financial support of the Canada Council for the Arts, the Government of Canada through the Canada Book Fund, and the Province of British Columbia through the British Columbia Arts Council and the Book Publishing Tax Credit.

Library and Archives Canada Cataloguing in Publication

Title: Un : poems / Ivan Drury.
Names: Drury, Ivan, author.
Identifiers: Canadiana 20210393734 | ISBN 9781772013764 (softcover)
Classification: LCC PS8607.R7495 U5 2022 | DDC C811/.6—dc23

*Dedicated to
Adel Hamad,
Omar Khadr,
and all the
disappeared*

1   Chainlink'd

9   Letters to Prison

13   Social Extract

18   Towards a Working Definition of "Un"

28   On Engels's *Dialectics of Nature*

31   K. to the Prison of Grass

35   Noise and the Stacking

49   Enter the Municipality of Blacksite
        (A Nuclear-Weapon-Free Zone)

61   The Body without Un

66   The Spectre of Apocalypse

75   Ore Memory

82   A Moment with the Cuban Section of the
        International (Stock Market)

85   In the Oranges and Whites

91   Che Guevara in his Dar es Salaam Hotel Room,
        after Withdrawing from the Congo Revolution

97   Geologies of Burning from the Sky and Centre

99   Lights Walls Metropoles

113 References

114 Acknowledgments

Chainlink'd

a spectre is haunting
negative space

extra
legal

a past
tense

four chainlink'd walls
bend it like
Bentham

extralegal
detention
alegal
extradition

"asymmetrical warfare"
PLUS
How many imperial gallons
VERSUS
How many litres
in a waterboard?
EQUALS
an un

a negative spectre
officially denied
an un

the photograph of Malcolm X
with his nose
inches from
       his Qur'an

represented his turn to
       "there's a worldwide revolution going on"

like the grotesque inverse:

the revolving
distended toes of Ali Abdullah Ahmed
Mani Shaman Turki al-Habardi Al-Utaybi
and Yasser Talal al-Zahrani

       inches from

dangling over
       their cell floor

their
       "asymmetrical war" against US-America

between Miami and the deep blue sea

do missing maps
equal missing lands?
do blankspots
over blacksites
under GoogleEarth
satellites?

between Miami and the deep blue sea
between Dakar and Mississippi

is there a Camp Echo in here?

does the parasite detain the host?

the whacking whistles to collect firewood
        to scare off the night
the whacking whistles to torture the interrogation

the master needs the slave

because the gun feels good
in your hands and
bad in your face

the moon-faced soldier with a naked man on a leash

a negative space
a genesis of negative life

a spectre
of waves
of Radio Swan

invisible and clanging

a distortion between the sea mist
and the terrible sun

I am casting off from Canada in search of un

as though my recognition could be a cure

I am on
a raft adrift
on an ocean of capital
Angelus Novus whirls and shows her fangs

A siren who summons
the twenty-thousand-league squid to surface
       tentacle'd
       beak'd
       sucker'd

monstrous
as I cling to my raft

seeking un or seeking to become un

the first coup attempt in Caracas
was five months
after 9/11

the failed coup in Bolivia
twenty months before the vacation from Kabul

Afghanistan took
one week to begin
and

imperial time-stamps a beginning but
refuses to end

involuntary exile
off the face

Nauru by freight
or Gitmo by blacksite

Letters to Prison

In the yard
we lie
on hammered earth
      to close the distance
      between soil and sky.

behind changes position
when position changes

there are
      prisons

behind speech acts
    memory acts
    up on
    anticipations
the hand stutters

in spaces without geographies
ice floats in dark water

the prisons
contract

In the yard
we jog

On the bars
we pull

our plain living body

      to close the distance
      between cell and blood

the body in prison
the body is prison
the body is in prison

the body is imprisoned
in the laws of present time
        suspended by behind bars

the LAWS OF HISTORICAL DEVELOPMENT
        fettered by capitalist relations of production

the LAWS OF PRODUCTIVE FORCES
        incarcerated people un-personed by mall cops with the
power of gods

the laws are
        tense and indeterminate

Social Extract

in my dreams
I am a mutant
superhero

and my power is
to storyboard the way things are being
silently   in secret

and without consequence

in waking life
I storyboard
the way things are being
secretly   in silence

and without consequence

but I am not a
superhero
and I do not have
any mutant powers

in my dreams

I dance with steel girders

without children

I dream of sex
with one forever

I watch MTV Canada
on the internet
in Vancouver

I watch MTV Russia
on TV
in Minsk

I watch MTV
in a bar near the train yard
in LA

I watch planes crash and crash and crash
on TV in a bar
on an island in the northern Pacific

on the docks workers move in
measured steps
and motions
to extract
exactly measured speed-up extant

the cranes impossibly overhead
spin from an axis
point
on the ground

a precise

point of contact
with the ground

through the concrete surface
with
the soil

dancing in workboots
not meant for dance
with people

meant to dance
the life
out of the necropolis
the dead capital
the polis of warehousing

    Wall Street versus Main Street tonight

extracted over all

in my dreams I

am a mutant superhero

dancing without joy

before cameras
choreographed and
without joy

Towards a Working Definition of "Un"

the seeing determines the scene

the light eater was hooded to
drop hood also over our heads

the seer determines the seen

the unseen the light eater

aboard a blacksite
a whiteman
waterboards
at fifty thousand feet

sustained by fuel plane
somewhere over the Pacific

un-torture
un-ended

the masked inquisitor calls an un-break
(labour laws still apply)

Lucy in the sky

        with indefinite detention

the masked inquisitor turns his back
on the hooded un
to pull off his mask and break the unity of anonymity
between untorturer and untortured

squinting, the unmasked inquisitor is faced with the outside glare
of a bare and swinging light bulb cliché
the stoic soldier's forearm hair stuck to forearm

anticipating the regret of the recalcitrant return to civilian life
he towels his arm undamp
the salt left after sweat might be
at least some proof

I am touched
there
for
I am

the smell of poverty

of unwashed pants

of sitting on the street

of waking up still drunk

and moving on

the sun still cold

the stair giving way

under gait

some bugs leak out

a spectre is haunting

    wherefore art thou haunting spectre
    will you renounce your haunting
    deny your communism

a spectre is a ghost

continents are contingent

cities are spectre

blacksites are

    LIGHT EATER

the police are stasis
a class-being of state-being
      of species-being suspended by uniform

a particular ripped from a totality

    a negative of un

in the eyes of fishes
air hides unknown depths
cement and steel
are
unchartable

wrecking reefs

the idea of *we* precludes

I am touched
there
for
I am

here
I am
asymmetrical
war

by unseeing

I am
a nation
of negative
space

born in atmosphere

spanked
until tears
draw breath

un born to be
asymmetry

Loneliness and boredom: these are the stepsisters of fear and panic. Unlike the latter they do not come upon one suddenly and savagely, but quietly and unexpectedly, usually after all the basic survival needs – water, food, shelter, and clothing – have been provided for. Loneliness and boredom can lead to depression and undermine the will to survive.

—*The U.S. Armed Forces Survival Manual*

On Engels's *Dialectics of Nature*

Beneath the rippling current
the stones lie still
piled in hills inverted
reaching, stretching deep into the
crust of the earth

Beneath the hard crack
crust of the earth

ripples the magma that
keeps its own tide

immune to the moon

A magnetic circuit
of molten iron
keeps the stream flowing
to the river

and from the river to the sea

an orienting polarity

The sun's light
colours the moving water
and its warmth draws it
into gas

The combustion of the sun's daily nuclear fusion
confronts the dark waters of the deepest craters of the
earth

as primary contradiction
as negation of negation

the purest synthesis of opposites
is humidity

K. to the Prison of Grass

K. moved to the prison of grass
from the occupied territories
de Girón
      through the corridors
of the arteries of the
      lines of
      passages

K. grew out his beard when
aging in detention allowed him

only by the grace of DoD go I

K. to the prison of grass from dust cometh

    K. have you heard
    in 2013 two Canadians in Egyptian prison
    were detained on terror or riot or anti-government conspiracy
    and were released finally on Canadian diplomat
    global power
    two partisans of the Palestinian cause
    made journalists and doctors by identification with Canada

    K. we told them

K. to the prison of grass from dust cometh

this new Canada is at once academic and trrrrtrrrrial
hard at the edges and marrow where the lives meet the days

pungent grey marrow

at the joints of these bones is
the lubrication of grinding contact

      K. have you heard
      my is not this state I renounce it
      this state is not my it holds me in the gentlest of tombs
      threatens me with salvation

We are all K.! say the journalist doctors in jets back to Canada

there is circulation of capital and
accumulation of land
in the corpreality

two Canadians in an Egyptian prison
must be released to never be
two Canadians in Millhaven prison
stateless in Guantánamo Bay
homeless incustody

Noise and the Stacking

whole notes
quarter notes
staccato
glottal
tremol
o

vehicle noise
refrigerator noise
machine noise
street light hum

breath
windtunnels
ear

what wind brings
what air

a shirtless without
piercing or tattoo

all parts
whole

vehicle noise
refrigerator noise
machine noise
the noise of street lights
either click or hum

pomade for the buzz of cityscape
whistle or hum

engines of varying sizes

in the east only the poor
whistle

a habit picked up along with
firewood

even bicycle wheels on streettop
how loud a pedestrian in the rain
overflow from headphones

there!
a voice expressing fear

another car alarm
police / fire / ambulance / police

we hear horror as testimony
that the fear is not ours
but we fear
being heard
as we hear:

                    afraid
                    and
                    at
                    least
                    a
                    block
                    away

the window

is only so violent as
its shattering
mimics a scream from a being

a mimesis of life
at its moment of destruction

      the paradox of a broken window
      is its proximity to revolt
      against the remedy of its insurance claim

who lures whose watch
to which
rock
on what ocean
disrupting whose course

wrecking even
the creative
urge to destroy

Plasticine body
without rectum or filth

the street noise of thought is desire

the bare mattress and your crawling skin

clothed in clean white sheet
sweat-yellowed pillow
some mould marks even
clothed in white clean pillowcase

digital
without filth

the smell of nothing
is a hint of scented bleach product
or the air from fantastic gardens
through a window just crack'd

the hospital bombed
over there
the staff had just cleaned the smooth surfaces with bleach

the gymnasium bombed
over there
the windows were tilted open near the ceiling
and from nearby you could hear the voices of children

trains on rails
not only the friction of motor
metal on metal rolling also
oil fume at point of production
smoke at point of contact
smoke at point of friction

consumption total

iron and mucus and lube

bellow and lung

small things
disappear in the giant's hand

hearing glass bones
embed these walls

such speed speeds thru
demands the illusion

of permanence

    why listen to a song again

overhead

an F-16

    and on the baby monitor:
    he's crying something's woken him
    shit and I was having such a good time

collapse

a window seen from the sky screen
spark rain zap on power lines
waves of radio pouring over satellite
the vacuumed silence of satellite
by design
the precision
the precise intelligent design

Enter the Municipality of Blacksite
(A Nuclear-Weapon-Free Zone)

The industrial centre
could not hold

from the deck of a freighter
on a sea without swell
Stanley Park is a hippie crown

perched on a financial forehead of glass

the bourgeoisie too recycles

the mayoral candidates
all wear "Homes Now!" buttons
all engage earnestly
on the side of the debate
to ban plastic shopping bags

I learned to ride a bicycle
on a street with chest-deep ditches
that froze in the winter
to skate, socks pulled over pant legs

first learned the way to a friend's house
two doors down
then school
then home became a place
day birthed beginning and end
then I became another
and learned to specify "my"

and "not my"

mother

dried blood mistaken for rust

Bagram does not buck its back
but shifts groaning
like an iceberg
or an ant colony behind glass

a hive of basements
burrow from cement stairwells
drills into sleep space

Charles Graner picks a hair from his wet tongue absently with his wire-rimmed glasses ridiculous moustache peaked hat absurd like a cliché WW II Nazi Jeremy Sivits testified that he watched Graner punch a hooded prisoner unconscious

history too erects signposts
"eighty years from Siberia"
to become it a place different
a Solzhenitsynist Tolkienite cloud world
never from we here

Bagram does not disappear
Guantánamo does not torture

no distance: no sign

where I grew up
we were all "middle class" and
everybody was "white"
at the time

where I grew up
families fell normally apart

drugs were not hard drugs

violence was not stranger violence

where I grew up
we named only those who were not where I grew up
our own bodies were unseen

I was trained in don't see colour

packed between the studs of our failed bourgeois family structure
and sealed with the drywall we painted with our fear

distance was insulation

there is no sign that says:

"You are now entering the municipality of Blacksite"

the un-spoken
is the rule

the un-naming of
names

the un-drawing of
maps

a junk train moving slow
through the plateau desert
passengers burrowed like ticks
on the back of an iron dragon
scales of rust or dried blood
T-shirts wrapped around our heads
against the sand sprayed by the rest of the world

until names ascribe things
drift into the spaces between characters
until spaces swallow maps
until mouths swallow speech

I saw the ghost of Bukharin again last night
scratching philosophy into his cell wall

we is vacuum

they is un

dead might be
at least some proof

The psychological antidote for loneliness and boredom is the same as for fear and panic: keep the mind occupied. Set priorities and tasks that will minimize discomfort, enhance the possibility of rescue, and provide for survival over an extended period of time. Consider unexpected yet possible emergencies as contingency operations and devise plans and tasks to deal with them.

Set a schedule. A schedule not only provides a form of security; it occupies the mind with the business at hand.

Loneliness and boredom can only exist in the absence of affirmative thought and action. In a survival situation there is always plenty of work that needs to be done.

—*The U.S. Armed Forces Survival Manual*

The Body without Un

The body
is scrap worked
into the form of a man

      a giant

The body
is a man who has a paper banner in the shape of a woman
he parades around Afghanistan

The hands of the giant are too large for the body of the giant

The hands are leathered by war
from strangling the land

because the giant is not of the land

The hands of the giant are memory
tanned by creosote
        creased by stretching iron rails over ties
        pocked by track-mark stitches

The giant's neck is a pedestal where the
universities perch
millions of minds

The body is a violent idea
made powerful by exclusion

here every negation is a membrane over the rotten hull
a deportation is caulking for a gap between mistaken boards
head taxes tar the starboard

The giant's tonsils hang like flypaper
dreams scream
caught in the throat of the nation

worker-spiders harvest what catches there
to edit and string code as glass beads

dead labour precludes
dead soldiers

lateral social division
the vertical consumption of exchange value

a soldier rides the precision-guided missile from a robot
flying through the bright Libyan sky into a pixel flash on
the lime-green screen from a trailer in the Vegas desert

a triumph of dead labour over the living
a fossil with a gun

a dried husk
a hardtack grave
an imprint with a clip

    a remote drone

        the body is dead labour
        with a gun

The Spectre of Apocalypse

The spectre of apocalypse is haunting
the spectre of communism

After twenty years the generals
took their claws off the Afghan pot
and the Taliban boiled over

The spectre of apocalypse
is a spitting boiling seething phantom
scalding all

with the guns of Nakba still flashing
the Soviets rushed to recognize the state of Israel

the monolith
dissolved
His fingernails
in vinegar

the monolith
prepared
His eggs
in vinegar

the monolith deemed
the extremities
expendable

is it for expediency the left can't see so Middle East?

Haifa Street is not the Ho Chi Minh Trail

the kufiyah conceals no gleaming red star

we love *The Battle of Algiers* more than the battles in Algiers

the militant is now
only un

the spectre of apocalypse
is the liberator whose terror
meets the horror of total living capital
in the chamber of total living empire

the only liberation we can imagine is from the total rule of living

    the militant
    he has joined the un

creating the notch where
needed

is the art of making strong
by parts
the whole

who touches
now the militant

un-monolithed
bombed
dislocated
declassed by militia-ization

what is class character

who touches now

and now who
still militant who

the spectre of apocalypse
has no folk songs
has poems only to remember
and organize genocide

has martyrs only to apocalypse

has no Victor Jara
to conduct handless the detained thousands
and raise soulful song
against fascism

the spectre of apocalypse
whirs out of an ark
of despair
all blades and teeth and chains

for decades we dreamed of a struggle on one front

for a crack in the hull of the great ship Party

but ours is a moment
of militant movement
without monolith

of currents without great ship
to breakwater

without eddies in time
for we flashing fishes to form against the riptide

ours is a militant who cannot see their hands

so quick is the current

so thick the blood

Ore Memory

in fifty years the tiles
fade

the passageways

the porcelain arch

the crease set
in your face

mama

as by iron
and board

beneath bronze
rusts metal
pores the cracks
the rains cry in

rust motion
is measured in mineral decay

ore osmosis is memory
falling or creeping out

must derrick
dock
derrick
dock

we too
lionize
only lions

the Taíno
revolutionary Cubans
set in bronze
in a swamp
in an alligator farm

our hearts are alternators
a real pain to change
the belt
        too tight

press the tip
of this pocket knife
into the leather
turn it
around around a round

beneath bronze
flows not blood
but rust

its motion
measured
in geologic time

we are
            through
            historical
            osmosis

the maps do not
make us
and we
do not
make the maps

I are or am not
we am or never will be

does today graph
above
or below history

does memory
trickle down into our hair
or must we draw
through derrick
through straw

beneath the crust of the earth
bleeds rock in reds

motion
not death

tracked in mineral decay

the fade on the tile
behind the common bath

we too
facing the sun

A Moment with the Cuban Section
of the International (Stock Market)

My father stands forlorn
on the Malecón

      In 1812 a Spanish galleon
      hit the reef out there where the waves break

he said

      dumped a hundred million dollars in gold bullion
      that's just sitting there on the ocean floor
      waiting to be found

he hoists me under arm
sandals and socks splashed with sea foam
released from whitecaps fifteen feet below

he points
his sleeve rolled past bicep
and faded tattoo

      there!
      you see where the waves are breaking?

my hair lay flat then
pasted by the humid wind of trucks passing
to my forehead

I look
past his target
to the east
the Morro Castle

and along the promenade
lovers far enough away
that I am not embarrassed to watch

the horn of a car behind us
sounds fuller
more
metallic
than the cars back home

the whole air an organism
electric

then
he lets me down

the sidewalk is hot
through the soles of my shoes

My new place is different definitely. People are generally nice, but with a lot of bad habits. Life here compels you to live like an animal because it is like a jungle. I have to change a little to defend myself, but not lose my humanity and who I am.

—Omar Khadr on moving to the Canadian Millhaven Institution from the Guantánamo Bay prison camp

In the Oranges and Whites

here near sky
casts far light

we watch the news
as proof

that we see

that we are the seers
not the scene

the crowd
is shapeless by design

shapeless and obsessed
with form

design divides: we from un

the prairies await the elevator
like the days await apocalypse

shapeless is the crowd
without militant

without knowing beginning
without anticipating end

apocalypse at the barrel of the gun is Daesh
apocalypse at the trigger of the gun is Michael Bay

a people without militant
is a population

when I was in high school
I walked at night
and spoke aloud
to myself

I stood on top
of water towers
reserve
water held in towers
in great containers
atop towers

I spoke aloud into the night

aloud and to myself

on a street
at night
in a fog
light is magnified
close and too bright

we are coming off
shift
and we are tired
and visible in

prison oranges
and
factory
whites

There aren't killer robots. There are unfeeling people behind the whole thing. There are some people who are extremely scary when talking to them. There was one person who had the word "infidel" tattooed on his arm in Arabic and had hellfire tattoos marking every shot.

—Brandon Bryant, former drone operator

Che Guevara in His Dar es Salaam Hotel Room, after Withdrawing from the Congo Revolution

After his retreat out of the Congo front Che Guevara
sequestered himself in a hotel room in Dar es Salaam and
wrote a critique of the war that began

    This is the story of a failure

the sun went down behind the blackout blind

Che had been drinking and sleeping

he was trying to read the section of *Capital* on machines
and factory laws

his eye was drawn to Marx's poetic and pessimistic
passages

he read over and over a pamphlet on chess strategy

Che had left his family in Havana saying

> if my children need shoes, the revolution will
> provide shoes or it will not

and

> I left behind ... a happy home if you can call the
> house of a revolutionary who is dedicated to his
> work a "home" – and a lot of kids who were
> barely aware of my love

he left his post with the revolutionary government after
the debate with Alberto Mora on the Soviet mechanism
of material levers in value production saying

> the blunt tools of capitalism will not make the
> socialist soul

when things were bad in the battle against the
Portuguese-backed forces some of the Cuban volunteers
reminded each other that Che had left his comfortable
home and important position behind to eat unsalted corn
cakes with them in the endless rain

Che asked the curtain pulled over his darkened window

Who am I now?

I felt alone, in a way I had never felt in Cuba nor
in any of my wanderings around the globe

Never have I felt myself so alone as I do today

the curtain did not answer

he felt that the African revolution had not failed but

I had not been equal to my responsibilities

As we rested on [a] hillside ... I reflected that
there were thirteen of us, one more than Fidel
had at a certain moment [in the Sierra Maestra
mountains] but that I was not the same leader he
was

let it rain
ragged and indiscreet

the end of the end
once the going stops

when discretion
the falling up sell fall
over the top of
under gutter

in
            dead leaves over
dead water

still stale stubborn

the under tow of
gravity in the tumbling

drops of ragged torn rain

we are revolutionary internationalists

no sky is foreign to us and no rain hostile

all people are our people
and nothing human is alien

no air is acrid
and no wind unwelcome

but what when the earth heaves against us and
our eager feet find no purchase

what when

Che slept and dreamed of the salt air that mists off the wave breaks on some trench mid-ocean – it was the Cayman Trough separating the Mexican coast from Cuba. He had a living memory wake him from his dream, of the thick humidity of the swamp that swallowed the blood of his comrades, the air so wet his skin felt like a tongue tasting the verdant living world that grumbled with hunger to consume him

when he woke he left for Bolivia where he found his death

the feeling that all is lost is always true

the conviction that victory is inevitable is correct

Geologies of Burning from the Sky and Centre

but north is no north
the sphere is skewed
polarity has relaxed and tensed
and will relax and tense again
in geologic time

I am held and hair smooth'd by this science
like laying in snow beneath competing spectres
dancing in the thick translucent sky

the sun a field
o'er the water
and the few islands

the world keeps no foreign sky

dust descends
partisans in the war against glass
merged of dust

what forms the foundations
of glinting glass
graveyards of the migrant
                              but dust

deep below
the dense
tenements of dust
it boils red pure like surface cannot know

this is essence too
who speaks of foreign soil
and its products
is entombed in their shoes
condemned to forever
finger words into breath on glass
the depths beyond
the particles of dust
the indistinguishable glass
reflecting back the dead soul

the window shows the face
that peers towards the light eater

Lights Walls Metropoles

The apocalypse cometh
The blanket kills
The revolution revolts
and all that is uttered drifts

The Abu Ghraib torturers have served their sentences
The "Union of Canadian Correctional Officers" proletarianizes

     under such global-force winds
     even steel evaporates

The vacuum howls
The tower mourns
bittersweet the song of separation

how well we

speak

Je me souviens *Rambo III*
the heroic mujahedeen

un hunger strikes for
a pair of shoes
a better blanket
visitation rights
medication

recognition

a pair
of shoes
a bet
ter blank
et vis
itat
ion rights
medi
cation
reco
gnition

"there can be no question of political status for
someone who is serving a sentence for crime
crime is
crime is
crime is crime"

shit is to Sands as suicide is to un

there is no jurisprudence without crime
there is warfare and

"assy
metri
cal warfare"

Dear Detainee #940

do you remember
buttery skin under your palm

do you wake up sick and stay in bed

do you dream of highways
or sores on your skin

do you lust

despite the glass at the corner at the crook of the
concrete ceiling and concrete walls and the
wire-cluttered window in the door

do you look at clocks
are there clocks anywhere
are there clocks everywhere

do you brush your teeth and floss

do you feel like watching TV is a waste of time
are there TVs anywhere
are there TVs everywhere

beneath such a hood
what memories
what projections

    lights

    walls

    metropoles

is it too loud at night
is it too quiet in the day

the triumph of form over content
of medium over message
is Rage Against the Machine
echoing loud in a cement cell

"fuck you, I won't do what you tell me"

constant dark and
constant light and
constant noise and
constant hum

occasional footfall and hinges creak

behold!

                  our dream cometh
                  without flag
                  without law
                  without nation-state

a
long intestine
spilling out of hand

behold!

                     the blacksite

a land
where
un is and cannot be

close my eyes
leave our lights on
I like the
fleshy glow

at the end of long days under
fluorescents
the lights will not leave my eyes
light worms move against sleep
loose fibres of the day

blankets kill

day
covers night

what spots of light

remembered
projected

beneath these hoods

behold!

a land
where
un is

References

The poems in *Un* contain quotes from the following documents:

Boswell, John, ed. *The U.S. Armed Forces Survival Manual.* New York: Times Books, 1980.

Costello, Norma. "Confessions of a Former US Air Force Drone Technician." Al Jazeera, April 13, 2016. www.aljazeera.com/features/2016/4/13 /confessions-of-a-former-us-air-force-drone-technician.

Democracy Now! "A Drone Warrior's Torment: Ex–Air Force Pilot Brandon Bryant on His Trauma from Remote Killing." October 25, 2013. www.democracynow.org/2013/10/25/a_drone_warriors_torment_ex_air.

Gálvez, William, and Ernesto Che Guevara. *Che in Africa: Che Guevara's Congo Diary.* North Melbourne, Australia: Ocean Press, 1999.

Guevara, Ernesto Che. *Congo Diary: Episodes of the Revolutionary War in the Congo.* North Melbourne, Australia: Ocean Press, 2011.

———. "On the Concept of Value: A Reply to Alberto Mora," in *New International* 8 (1991).

Marsh, Heather. "Omar Khadr: War Criminal, Child Soldier … or Neither?" *Vice News*, September 25, 2013. www.vice.com/en/article/yvqznx/omar -khadr-war-criminal-child-soldier-or-neither.

Risen, James, and Tim Golden. "3 Prisoners Commit Suicide at Guantánamo." *New York Times,* June 11, 2006. www.nytimes.com/2006/06 /11/us/11gitmo.html.

Turse, Nick. "The Pentagon's Planet of Bases." Tom Dispatch, January 9, 2011. tomdispatch.com/nick-turse-the-pentagon-s-planet-of-bases/.

Acknowledgments

Un was written on the unceded and occupied Territories of the Leq'á:mel Nation, and on the unceded and occupied Territories of the xʷməθkʷəy̓əm, Sḵwx̱wú7mesh, and səĺilwətaʔɬ Nations. The occasional pessimism that runs through these ruminations about imperialism, socialism, and apocalypse is defied by the living refusal of settler colonialism modeled by these Indigenous Nations through their defiance of Canada's genocide and their sovereign decolonial resurgence.

I first wrote *Un* as a long poem in December 2007, after a long and intense period of organizing against the beginning of a new period of imperialist aggression, defined by the US-led occupation of Iraq and Canada's occupation of Afghanistan. As I prepared the poem to be published, fourteen years later, the US was performing its catastrophic defeat and evacuation from Afghanistan – which has not meant the end of US imperialism. The original poem I wrote in 2007 has been significantly modified by developments in the years since, but I have decided to keep the accents of each particular historical moment intact. Some of the references in this poem are historical marks and might not be immediately familiar to a contemporary reader.

For me, the writing of this poem bookended a long and difficult decade that included a constant push-pull between my obligations to the practical daily work of political organizing and my always-less-urgent commitment to literary work. Without the support and encouragement of my friend Cecily Nicholson, it is inconceivable that this manuscript would ever have been finished, let alone published.

Jeff Derksen, Clint Burnham, and Wade Compton welcomed me into their classrooms and workshops as an unknown (and surely disagreeable) auditor, and they introduced me to a world of poetry richer than I imagined existing. Earlier versions of some of these poems were published in *West Coast Line* and performed at the Positions Colloquium in 2008 with the support of Andrea Actis.

I owe a debt of gratitude to Catriona Strang at Talonbooks who pulled the poem into final shape, finding my inconsistencies, oversights, and errors with a keen, careful eye. Thanks to Stephen Collis for a last-minute read-through.

Thanks also to my comrades in the Red Braid Alliance for Decolonial Socialism and my co-editors at the *Volcano* newspaper. I remember my beloved community members murdered by colonialism and capitalism during the years this poem was written, including Linda Mama Bear Whitford, Little Joe Bauman, Richard Cunningham, Jodie Buckaneer, Stevie Ray, Tina James, Tracy Morrison, Denise Richards, and countless others I cannot name.

Finally, thank you to my friends and loved ones who believe in me and support and encourage me to write: Nadine, Listen, Mom, Dad – and most of all, Stacey, always.

Ivan Drury is a founding member of Red Braid Alliance for Decolonial Socialism and editor and writer with the *Volcano* newspaper. He has a long history in leftist communities on the unceded Territories of the xʷməθkʷəy̓əm, Sḵwx̱wú7mesh, and səl̓ilwətaʔɬ Nations. Ivan has a master's degree in history from Simon Fraser University and teaches history and labour studies to international students. *Un* is his first book of poetry.